My Journey, His Plan

by
Sharon Shymansky Roberts

My Journey, His Plan
Copyright © 2015
Sharon Shymansky Roberts

All rights reserved. This publication may not be reproduced, stored in a retrieval system, or transmitted in any form: recording, mechanical, electronic, or photocopy, without written permission of the publisher. The only exceptions are brief quotations used in book reviews

Comments:
Contact Sharon Shymansky Roberts
Email - shroberts164@gmail.com
www.facebook.com/

ISBN: 978-1-941069-33-2

Published by ProsePress
Pawleys Island, South Carolina 29585

www.ProsePress.biz
proseNcons@live.com

Dedication

This book is dedicated to my two loves, David and Dan. The first loved and married the young woman I was and gave me the three greatest treasures of my life, our sons. The second took the widowed shell of an older woman and gave her the wings to fly and grow.
I owe you both all that I am today.
My love for you is eternal.

I Know You

In Sunday School I sang songs
About You.
Each time I sang I proclaimed my love for You.
You lived in my heart
And
I was safe in the promise of Your words.
A child of pure innocence,
I knew You.

In my waning youth, I prayed to You.
But you appeared to have taken up residence in others' hearts,
Deserting mine for richer, more fertile soil
To plant Your seeds.
I truly believed I opened my heart to You,
But my mind would cling to provoking conversations,
Disturbing dialogues, misunderstood theology,
Leaving me to question.
Leaving me to doubt.
I thought I knew You.

Older still, beauty found in Your landscapes invigorated me.
Births and deaths I witnessed were but backdrops to Your presence.
It was You,
In each scene, each event,
Inspiring me to embrace You again.
Once blocking You with my doubt,
Silencing You with my mistrust,
With each day I lived, each place I went,
I began to know You were there.

Now, in my sunset years, my heart is open,
And You are filling me with Your presence.
Molding me.
Saving me.
Loving me.
Inspiring me.

So thankful,
Because,
Now, I truly know You.

Written by Sharon Shymansky Roberts and Pat David

My Journey, His Plan

by
Sharon Shymansky Roberts

Prose Press

Contents

	Introduction	1
1.	First Day of School	5
2.	Evil Intent	9
3.	The Homecoming	17
4.	Almost Perfect Love Story	27
5.	A Love Letter to Cobb Island	35
6.	Along for the Ride	39
7.	The Power of Faith, Family, and Friends	43
8.	Alpacas and... Dragonflies?	49
9.	Tourist Eyes	53
10.	Expect the Unexpected	55
11.	If He Calls... Answer!	59
12.	God's Plan	63
	Acknowledgments	69

Introduction

I am a 60-something retired English teacher. Every English teacher I have ever known wants to write a book, usually the great American novel. I just want to write. I have always wanted to write and have done it sporadically through the years. Most of it I saved, hence "the folder" you will later read about. I seldom shared what I wrote, unless you count the times in junior high when I was Jimmy's campaign manager as he ran every year for class president. I wrote all his speeches and they were ebullient, mostly because I "loved" him so much! He won every campaign and was convinced it was because of my writing ability.

So I continued to write, mostly about events that inspired me. Many of them were simple, every day experiences where I began to recognize God's hand in my plan. At age 22, I met David, and life was never the same. He was an Adonis and a sweetheart, and I fell hard when our mothers introduced us. Three sons and 26½ years later, he fell victim to cancer due to exposure to Agent Orange in Vietnam, and died. I remember thinking that if there was to be no more love in my life after David, it was okay, because most women never get to be loved the way I was loved by him. But God and David weren't done with me, and they sent me Dan. David's family and mine loved Dan as well and, soon, we married.

Not long after, I found alpacas and fell in love once again. I jumped when a chance to buy land, build a farm, and start raising these animals presented itself. Dan jumped right alongside me and Camillo Valley Alpacas was born. For ten years we raised God's perfect livestock. We loved our alpaca life, but ten years is a long time when you were 50-something at the start. Retirement loomed.

Spring break would often find us guests of some of our dearest friends, renting a beach house with them in Litchfield Beach, South Carolina. On an exploring expedition one year, Dan and I found Pawleys Island beach, and we knew where we would live when we retired. In December, 2013, we sold our farm and became residents of Pawleys Island.

Retirement has afforded me time to return to my love of writing, and it has provided me the inspiration to do so. Maybe I am aware I am getting closer to the time God will call me home, and so I seek Him more, or maybe there is an inspiration in the sand and salt water that is calling to me, but I seem to be more attuned to God' s presence in my daily life than ever before.

I am writing this book now because it has taken this long for me to trust and believe that I am doing God's will. He tried to tell me to write for Him so many times along my journey. I remember once, in my early 30s, I had the urge to write a novel. It was all planned, chapter by chapter. But I was afraid. So, after reading Og Mandino's book, *The Greatest Salesman in the World*, for the third time, I decided to test God. I wrote a letter to Og Mandino telling him about the novel that was inside of me trying to get out. On the envelope I wrote, "First novel erupting within. Frightening experience. Help." I actually sent the letter and told God I would write the book if Mr. Mandino responded. Well, he responded. He was in the middle of writing a book, a time when he'd never normally read his mail. But the envelope was intriguing, and it was obvious I hadn't sent him a manuscript to read, so he opened my letter, and he wrote back. He wrote that it was obvious I could write and to go do it! It's 30 years later now, and I'm just beginning to take his advice. How sad. Another promise to God broken. Rather than trusting in Him and stepping out on faith, I let fear of failure and rejection keep me in the shadows all that time. Over and over I have heard that you only fail when you fail to try. Hearing it and believing it are sometimes two different things. But I believe it now, and I am tired of failing.

But what about you, the reader? What do I want for you? I want to touch you. I want to open your eyes to the presence of the Lord in your tragedies, in your joyous moments, and in your everyday normal existence. I want you to see Him all around you and feel His love. When you open yourself up to the possibility of finding God traveling with you every minute of every day, it's humbling and it's exciting, and it's the beginning of building an even stronger relationship with your Lord. That's what I want for you!

The First Day of School

I believe God gives each of us specific talents He expects us to use in His name to serve His people. I believe, based on those talents, He calls us to a service and a career. Often, He calls us early, sometimes way too early for us to even understand the call. But He continues to call. I got "the call" when I was in third grade. It was about that time I began setting our boxer puppies, one at a time, in my younger sister's high chair so I could teach them, using my chalkboard, all about whatever I was learning in school. I knew then I was going to be a teacher and, except for a brief time of wanting to be an Olympic equestrian, I never strayed. It was something I knew I was called to do. God is calling. Are you listening?

School began today. Once again I awoke resentfully from a sound slumber to the tuneless jangling of my mechanical rooster. Once again I tiptoed silently into two bedrooms to kiss three sleeping sons "hello" and "goodbye." Once again I stood courageously before the room stuffed with 30-some less than captivated adolescents, and I wondered why, after 13 years of teaching, I still have butterflies in my stomach on the first day of school.

I suppose it's largely anticipation, perhaps a tad of curiosity, and just a pinch of suspense. Though experience has taught me anything can happen in a classroom (and usually will during the course of a year), there are still some things that are predictable. For instance, it is a certainty that before the next 10 months expire, I will have fallen irrevocably in love with at least three of those anxious, arrogant faces. Some five or six more will become friends I will, with gentle coaxing, eventually recall 10 years from now when I meet them in the store. And one or two will come readily to mind often in the years ahead because I will worry about them, and wonder how I could have helped them more. Should I have done this? Could I have done that? Did I fail them when they needed me? Anger. Worry. Guilt. Joy. Love. Excitement. Oh, the feelings this schoool year will bring!

The feelings. The torn feelings. Free this past summer weeks from the pressure of too much to do in too little time; free from the guilt of neglecting my family for my career and, on some days, my career for my family; free from the intense mental labor necessary to reach the educational needs of 90-some students day after day, five days a week, I still continued to eagerly anticipate today's arrival.

Why can't I be content to stay at home as a full-time mother to my three sons and a full-time wife to my loving husband? Why must I continue to teach? It can't be the money. No one willingly goes through so much for so little. It's me. There's something in me that brings me back each year despite my sworn oath, muttered solemnly every mid-June, that I am laying down my markers and red pencil forever, and this time I really mean it!

No, it's in me. Nowhere else do I feel so needed by so many. I am their teacher, but I have a God-given talent for becoming their friend as well. My students trust me, confide in me, listen to me. I need that. I need to feel I play an important role in their lives for the 10 months we are together. Anyone can come in and teach from a textbook, but good teaching is so much more than that! Good teaching means going beyond the curriculum and giving a little of myself each day to whoever needs me for whatever reason. It means being involved in their lives and helping them make decisions they can live with, as they face situations they are certain they can't live through.

But… I am needed at home, too. Two small guys hurry home from school full of eager tales to tell, but Mom isn't home and tale telling doesn't wait. Meanwhile, one smaller guy plays quietly all day with the sitter and constantly queries, "Is it time for Mom yet?" And the most special guy in the universe must be content with what is left of me each day after I have cried, laughed, scolded, cajoled, threatened, and bargained (all under the guise of teaching) innumerable times during the 10 hours since he last saw me. Why do I do this to him? Why do I do this to me? Is teaching so important?

And so it begins. The contest. The struggle. The inner turmoil that will pull and tug at the very essence of me all through this school year, until the afternoon of the last day of school, when I will meander exhaustedly down deserted hallways weakly proclaiming the end of my teaching career once again, but fooling no one, as usual. I will return… I will return… Dedicated teachers always do.

Evil Intent

Have you ever been in an extremely dangerous situation and come out unscathed? Did you wonder why God saved you when so many other people in similar situations are not as fortunate? It is in those times that I am strengthened by the fact God has a plan for me, and He is not done with me yet.

It was late afternoon. I had finished teaching my middle school students for the day and needed to stop in the drugstore on my way home. Parking not far from the door, I approached the entrance, noticing a group of teenage boys hanging around the front of the store. Some of them I had taught when they were sixth-graders. I remembered the faces, but not the names.

"Hey, Mrs. Shymansky, what's happening?" a voice queried.

"Hey, guys. How are you today?"

"Good. Good. It's all good. How's Sgt. Shymansky?"

"He's fine, guys. Still working those crazy shifts!"

I remember thinking how odd the question about my police officer husband was, considering it was followed by a strange look that passed between two of the boys.

"Okay, then. Let me get my shopping done. Have a great afternoon," I commented as I strode into the store. Once inside, I immediately noticed one of my colleagues, Bill, shopping just inside the door at the bargain table.

"Hi, Bill. You have a honey-do list before you get home, too, huh?"

"Always, Sharon. Always. How was your day today?"

"Oh, it was fine. That third period class is enough to tweak my last nerve, though. I think you have them fifth period. They are certainly a lively bunch!"

"No they aren't! They're hoodlums, just like those yahoos hanging out front of the store. Not a motivated bone among 'em!"

Laughing, I retorted, "Oh my! Somebody *did* have a bad day! Well, let me find what I need and get down the road to collect my own hoodlums! I'll see you tomorrow!"

As I exited the store a few moments later, I had the creepy feeling that the boys still hovering by the door were waiting for me. "Hey, Mrs. Shymansky," one of them called out, "you remember that baseball book you used to read to us at the end of class? Man, that was a good book. I liked it when you read to us." This was being said as the boys moved in closer, almost forming a semicircle in front of me, blocking my path to the parking lot. No sooner had my heart rate started to accelerate than, as if on cue, the boys parted as another joined the crowd. Meanwhile, Bill had noticed the circle of boys and had come to my rescue.

"Hey, boys, don't you have some place important to be? Let the lady, through."

I hurried to my car, a little shaken by the experience. Something evil had been in the air. Quickly stashing my purchases in the back seat, I started the car and exited the parking lot. One left turn onto Route 6, a right turn onto Route 301, and I was headed home to the serenity of Cobb Island. The speedometer began climbing to the 55 mile an hour speed limit. I set the cruise control and settled in for the 30 minute ride home. Suddenly, the steering wheel began vibrating in my hands. The vibration quickly accelerated to the point I could barely keep the car on the road. The shaking seemed to come from the front passenger wheel, and I remember thinking, "I must have a hell of a flat tire!" as I slowed the car and tried to guide it to the shoulder. I could barely move the steering wheel, it was vibrating so wildly. Just holding on was the best I could do! As I was attempting to maneuver the car, I heard a siren to my left and someone shouting on a microphone, "Stop the car! Stop the car!" I could see in my side view mirror the black and white of a county police car.

    I braked. My car, which had slowed considerably, stopped almost immediately. I began shaking as badly as the steering wheel had. The police car screeched to a stop behind me. I rolled down my window as the officer approached. Before he got to me, however, I noticed a second police car, lights flashing, siren blaring, speeding my way. I knew my husband was on day shift, and I began praying it was him rushing to my rescue. "Please God, please God. I need David!" Sure enough, when the second police car skidded to a halt in front of me, my handsome husband came flying out of the car. He ran immediately to my window while the other police officer slowly roamed around my car, carefully inspecting every wheel. "Oh my God, Sharon, are you okay? What the hell happened?" Still sitting behind the steering wheel, I began sobbing. "It's all right, honey. Don't cry. Everything's all right now. Just sit tight a minute."

    I heard David converse quietly with the other police officer, then both of them slowly circled the car while the first officer pointed downwards to various places on both sides of

My Journey, His Plan

my car. David returned to my window. "Okay, honey. I want you to gently ease yourself out of the car. I'll help you." He slowly opened the car door and reached for my hand. Sliding out gently was not an easy feat considering my entire body was shaking uncontrollably, and I was still crying. "It's okay, baby. It's okay," as he drew me from the car and enveloped me in his arms. We stood entwined on the side of the road until my shaking and crying stopped. "Okay, that's better. Now, we need some information, Sharon, and I have to show you something that's going to upset you. I want you to be brave." That comment was almost enough to start me sobbing again, but I held it together.

Grabbing my hand, he walked me to the front passenger side of the car. My eyes were immediately drawn to the front tire. The entire wheel of the car was balanced precariously on the very edge of the axle. There were no lug nuts to be seen. I understood immediately that I had been a millisecond away from having the entire wheel fall off my car! Instantly I envisioned what could have happened. The car veering uncontrollably on the road as the wheel dropped off; my car smashing into other vehicles, turning over, flinging me onto the road. Innocent people killed. Even me. I shuddered and felt sick to my stomach. "Honey, look at me," as he grabbed both my shoulders and turned me to face him. "Someone deliberately loosened all the lug nuts on all four wheels. We need to know who did this. It had to have happened a short time ago, because you couldn't have driven from school with your wheels like this. Where did you stop?"

"I… I was at the CVS. There were some boys there. I used to teach a couple of them, but I can't remember their names. I don't know – there were maybe six, seven of them.

I think they're all in high school now. They spoke to me, and they asked about you. I don't know their names. I can't even think right now! Oh… wait a minute, Bill, Bill Stevens. He works with me. He was there. I think he knows them. Maybe he can tell you who they are."

"Okay, hon. You did fine. Now, I'm going to send you home with Private Scott. Go take care of our boys. Are you going to be okay?"

"Yes. I'll be fine. What are you going to do?"

"I'm going to do my job. I'll call you later."

Several hours later he finished his shift and returned home, without my car. Dinner and his boys were waiting for him, so it wasn't until bedtime that we got to talk. "So… did you find anything out today?"

"I did. It's not anything I can talk about."

"What do you mean you can't talk about it? I could have been killed today! I think I have a right to know everything that's going on. And where's my car?"

"The car's in the shop being checked. I want to make sure everything's okay with it. It was at the crime lab most of the day being dusted for prints."

"And did they find any?"

"Again, it's not anything I can talk about." This time it was spoken in that tone that means, "Don't talk to me about this again." So I shut up.

The next day at school, though, puzzle pieces began falling into place. Bill and I shared a common planning period, and he was eager to bring me news. "Your husband was at my house late yesterday afternoon. One minute I'm reading the paper, and the next minute my doorway is filled with this really tall, really well-built police officer! Man, how tall is he? He must be 7 feet tall! Does he work out? His arms are huge? Boy, was he mad!" Barely stopping for breath, he continued, "So those boys loosened all your lug nuts, huh? I told you they were hoodlums! I knew them all, every one of them. I gave him *all* their names. Boy, are they going to be in trouble! Wait until he shows up at their houses! There's gonna be some crappin' in the pants all over the county!"

I don't know how prophetic Bill's last statement was, but apparently, part of it was true. David did show up at all of their homes. Police officers and their wives, especially in a small county with a small police department at the time, are a pretty tight knit group, so it wasn't surprising that one of the wives dropped in to see me a few days after the incident. After the small talk, she got around to her real reason for visiting. "Sharon, I heard about your incident. That must have been terrifying! Aren't you glad the boys weren't in the car? And to think what could have happened if that wheel had come off! It's just plain scary. And they did this in broad daylight? It's crazy. Crazy!"

"It was pretty frightening," I responded, not really wanting to relive it.

"I hear David was pretty determined. You know, he and Scotty visited every single boy's home. He took Scotty as a witness so no one could accuse him of harassment or anything, but he sat with every family. Scotty told his wife that your husband was amazing! He sat with their parents and the boys, and he apparently explained in graphic detail what happened and what could have happened. He even outlined to the parents what they could have been facing had the events turned out differently. He talked about their families and questioned how they might feel if one of them had to experience what you had. Boy, Scotty said he never heard anything like it. He said the boys had to feel lower than worms when he was done. He loves you so much, girl!"

This was the first I had heard of the visits, though knowing David as I did, I had expected as much. The fact that he didn't tell me himself didn't surprise me. All he had said was that it was taken care of, and for me not to worry. David was very good at this kind of calm, empathetic confrontation, but it must have taken all his willpower to stay in control during those visits.

Weeks later, David did share with me that it was just one young man who loosened the lug nuts; all the others had succumbed to peer-pressure to keep me busy while he did the deed. That one young man, David admitted, had a grudge against him from a prior arrest, and he was seeking revenge. Not long after this incident, the young man made another poor decision and got into serious trouble. This time, he was no longer a juvenile, and justice was served.

God saved me that day, and I was very grateful, but I think He used David to save some young boys who might have chosen a different path if not for this incident. Even horrifying events, it seems, can be part of God's plan, and good can come from evil.

The Homecoming

I have many friends born in other countries who have intentionally chosen to live in the United States. Every one of them says the same thing, repeatedly. "You have no idea how lucky you are to have been born here. This is the best country in the world, even with its imperfections." Thank you, God, for allowing me to be born and live in the USA. I am forever grateful. Please continue to bless this country; we need You.

It is not important who I am, only what I have become this night. And even that is not as important as what has just transpired in this coliseum before the eyes of nearly 20,000 people of all ages, races, and religions. Tonight, many thousands of us came closer to understanding the true character of the American spirit that made and has kept our country free. We began to comprehend our God-given rights, as well as our inherited responsibilities. But above all, we discovered that freedom is not free; there is always a price to be paid.

The sudden insights did not come tonight from knowledge learned and immediately digested by the brain, but rather from events that purged and enlarged our hearts. How fitting such a phoenix-like transformation in our attitudes should rise from the ashes of our nation's greatest humiliation.

He stood proudly erect at the podium, his feet disappearing mysteriously into a peaceful mass of red, white, and blue balloons. Rows of multi-colored ribbons and glistening medals applauding past achievements contrasted with the background of his Marine Corps dress whites. He was an impressive figure, yet the price he had paid was painfully obvious.

A loan, black patch ominously covered his left eye socket. The eye itself had long since decayed on a solitary hill in Vietnam. His right hand was pitifully misshapen from attempting to protect his eyes from an enemy grenade. He had neither left hand nor left arm. Those ashes reside on the same hill, as do bits and pieces of both legs, a shoulder, and his neck. Yet, Lt. Clebe McClary stood smiling before us tonight, calm and serene, overflowing with the joy he had found in serving the Lord since his return from Vietnam and his 2½ year hospital recovery.

The lieutenant briefly recounted the Vietcong attack that cost him so dearly, his lengthy recovery, and his acceptance of the Lord, not to preach to us as much as to prove, "Ask and ye shall receive." Lying in shattered pieces in a foreign land several years ago, he had asked, no, begged to live to see his men go home alive and to see his beautiful wife one more time. The Lord had listened; both requests had been granted.

As soul-stirring as his story was, Lt. McClary was not the reason my country found my heart tonight, though he was the instrument. After his brief oration, he invited all World War II, Korean, and Vietnam vets to walk across the stage so he could shake their hands, brother to brother.

Twenty thousand people rose, hands clapping in polite appreciation, as graying World War II and Korean veterans walked proudly across the stage, accepting gracefully the homage we paid them. They seemed pleased and touched but, after all, they had been heroes and had been through all this before. Tickertape parades. Victory celebrations. The proud return of our brave fighting men. It was pleasant, I'm sure, for them to remember back to other homecomings.

Not so for the Vietnam vets. They were different – obviously different. As they began their march across the stage, the applause crescendoed into a deafening thunder that reverberated throughout the coliseum. It must have been music to their ears. I found myself mysteriously called to leave my seat and stand at the lower end of the stage. I watched the face of each veteran as he shook hands with Lt. McClary. Many faces were tear-streaked, eyes alive with relived horrors, grief, and pain. Others appeared relaxed and grateful, as if a great burden had suddenly been lifted. Nearly all their faces shown with a resurgence of the pride they had once felt, long ago, in what they had done. Each man stepped quickly off the stage, many turning immediately to embrace another – instant brothers, though unknown all these years – tied together by an unforgettable bond. Each man had been willing to give his life for a country that had turned her back on him. While other veterans returned from their wars to elaborate homecomings and a thankful America, Vietnam vets had been spit on, cursed at, and denied their rights. They had lived a hell, fighting far from their homeland in a war they weren't even allowed to win.

Like other veterans before them, they had watched

their brothers and friends die. They had seen war at its worst, and it had left its mental mark. Some of them, like Lt. McClary, had even left a part of themselves behind. But there was no homecoming – until tonight. No fanfare – until tonight. No thank you's – until tonight. Tonight belonged to them. They relished in it. They wept in the face of it, and the raw wounds of past rejections started to heal.

Yes, tonight a small portion of America's fighting men were partially repaid for their allegiance, but 60,000 of her boys never made it to any homecoming. They never came home. And they were not the only war casualties. In the years since the war's end, another several thousand Vietnam vets have committed suicide. Many thousand more developed various cancers as a result of Agent Orange. What a price America has paid!

And yet, tonight I am so proud to be of the same flesh and blood as those parading in front of me. Only America, the originator of freedoms that are but whispers of hope to most of the world, could inspire such loyalty, devotion, and pride. These Americans before me fought to keep the idea of "free men" alive. No matter whose soil or people, when the cry for freedom goes up, Americans will be there, for "to whom much is given, much is expected." God has blessed America with everything man has ever craved, and great is our responsibility to the rest of mankind because of those blessings.

Tonight, I truly became an American. The spirit of the people who have fought to defend her ideals reached into my soul and shattered its apathy. Freedom is not free; it never has been. It never will be. America will pay the price again, and again, and again, here and on foreign soil as well. But freedom is like an expensive, fine wine – once tasted, one can never be satisfied with a bargain brand.

While I stand and applaud these Vietnam vets, like those around me are doing, I pray a thankful prayer that they were willing to do what had to be done, that they were there to answer freedom's call, and that there are others like them waiting, ever ready, to keep the eagle flying free.

Thirty Years Later...

"The Homecoming" was written about 30 years ago, immediately after attending this event. It lay in my writing folder (a simple manila folder with handwritten stories) all those years. When we moved here to Pawleys Island, the folder came with us, though it was once again stuffed in my night table next to my bed. When God made it clear He wanted me to write this book, He sent me to the folder. I had truthfully forgotten about it, but three times, in my frustration about "what else am I supposed to write," I was told to look in the folder. I did what I was told. Each time I passed over this story, not thinking it would fit. Each time He sent me back. The last time, I sat on my bed with all the stories laid out before me, and I asked for His help. "Why are you sending me back here again, Lord? What is it I am supposed to see?" Carefully I looked at each of my writings. I returned story after story to the folder. When I picked up this story off the bed, a peace settled inside me. The frustration disappeared. "OK, I get it, Lord. I'll use this one, but I don't why."

I immediately gave the story to my husband to read. He had been in Vietnam, and I thought he could tell me if he thought it was a good fit for the book. As he was reading, he began tearing up and couldn't finish the story right away. He looked up at me with moist eyes and said, "It's good, honey. It really is, but I have to take a minute and catch my breath. It's pretty emotional." I remember thinking that maybe I had something there. I decided right then to look up Lt. Clebe McClary to see if he was even still alive. I grabbed my phone and did a google search while Dan returned to his reading. I found the Lieutenant's website right away and clicked on it. I read all about him and his ministry, happy to see he had continued, in a big way, to serve the Lord. At the bottom of the page it said, "Click here for more information," so I did. It took me to a contact page, and there the goosebumps started and the hair on the back of my neck truly did stand up. I read the address, a post office box in Pawleys Island, SC, my new home! I started crying at this point, because it became very obvious to me that God really wanted me to use this story, though I still had no idea why. "Oh my gosh, Dan, you aren't going to believe this!" and I shared the address with him, tears streaming down my cheeks.

"No way, Sharon! What the heck is going on?"

"I have no idea, but I know God wants me to use this story, and I know I have to contact Lt. McClary to get his permission to use it." Not being one to waste time when I am truly excited, I called the phone number and left a message on the recording. Not satisfied with that, I sent an email to the contact person on the ministry website. I slept very little that night.

The next morning I went to my exercise class early and called a few of the ladies into a huddle with me. "Ok, girls. Some of you have lived here a lot of years. I need to know if you know anyone who knows Clebe McClary," and I briefly explained my book and why I needed Lt. McClary's permission.

"Oh my Gawd," my friend Liz exclaimed. "He's just about my husband's oldest friend. They went to grade school together and everything! You just contact that person on the website and tell 'em you are a friend of Humdinger's wife!" Now, all of us had goosebumps. Something was at work here I couldn't understand.

That weekend Liz and her husband came to a get-together at our house, and I gave them a copy of the story. Liz folded it up and put it in her purse. I will be forever grateful to Glen (Humdinger) for two things: (1) That night he lent me his copy of Deanna McClary's book, *Commitment to Love*. It was "the rest of the story" about their love, Clebe's time in Vietnam, the beginning of their ministry, and her story of faith and courage as she stood beside Clebe through all his trials. It's an emotional and uplifting story every woman who has ever loved should read. (I cried my way through it that weekend!) And number 2? The next morning, Glen read my story and took the next step for me.

The morning after our get-together, an excited Liz called me. "Sharon, Glen read your story this morning and got right on the phone and called Clebe! Guess what? Deanna answered and she said she'd tell Clebe all about it and how you want to use it in your book. She said she can't wait to read it!" The McClary's don't just witness for the Lord in this country, they do it worldwide, and the fact that even one of them was home was a miracle to me.

I just got a call from Liz tonight, and tomorrow I am meeting Lt. Clebe McClary. If you are reading this story, then you know I was granted permission. But there's an even more important reason I will not sleep tonight. This is a man the Lord chose. He asked Clebe to use his pain and suffering as an instrument to reach out to others and bring them to

Him to be healed. Clebe listened and did as he was asked. Courage on the battlefield. Courage in the aftermath. Courage to witness for Him. I will be humbled to even be standing in his presence.

The Meeting...

Dan and I were early. I was nervously anticipating the meeting. This was a big deal. While my simple little essay had lain in my writing folder all those years, this man, along with his wife, had become evangelists known all over the world. And I was about to meet him.

"Here he is," Glen called out, and he opened the door to let Clebe in. This time in shorts, a red tee shirt with a Marine Corps emblem, and flip flops, he looked much less intimidating than in his dress whites. Thank goodness! Introductions were made and I handed him my story, asking for his permission to use it in my upcoming book. Liz suggested we all sit at the dining room table to discuss this. We did, and Clebe ended up sitting to my left.

He fumbled through the pages of my story, turning them over and mumbling, "Oh my, it's long. Ummm, Sharon. I think I would like it better if you read the story to me." How could I forget – his eye patch! I'm sure the small type in my story would challenge him. But read to him?

I can't do that, I thought. I can't read a story to him about his body parts being blown all over Vietnam. What if I send him back into some kind of post-traumatic stress? But I just smiled and said, "Sure."

One of the talents God gave me is the ability to be a dramatic reader, which is one of the reasons I am a lector at church. I believe in giving back. Anyway, I read. When I got to the "blown up body" part of the essay, I placed my hand on his arm, and kept reading, tiny sobs breaking my voice here and there. Halfway through, I had to stop and take a breath. "I'm sorry, sir, but if you had told me 30 years ago that someday I would be reading this story to you, I would have called you a liar. I'm having a hard time believing this is really happening."

"Keep reading, Sharon. You're doing a great job."

By the time I finished the last two sentences, I was in a full blown cry, but I was not alone. Liz jumped up and handed everyone Kleenex! "Well, I can tell you this. You, young lady, can write! That was very well done, and I am honored you wrote about me. You may use this story whenever and however you like." There it was. Permission granted. We spent the next half-hour chatting about all sorts of things, and Clebe mentioned that we would all have to get together at his house so I could meet Deanna. He was due to fly to Dallas the next day, but he would be in touch soon. And then he left. I spent the rest of the day in a euphoric state. He had liked it, really liked it! I was happy.

Early the next morning my phone rang. When I answered, a male voice boomed out, "What in the world are you doing with a Maryland phone number, girl?"

"I'm sorry, who is this?"

"It's me, Clebe! I just wanted to tell you how much I enjoyed meeting you and Dan yesterday. I told Deanna all about it, and she can't wait to meet you. I just want you to give us until all this craziness dies down. Maybe by mid-August, we can have you guys over here. I really want to get to know you both better!"

"Clebe, aren't you supposed to be in Dallas today?"

"Yep. On my way to the airport now, but I just had

to call you and tell you that we're gonna get together, and I can't wait."

"Okay then. I can't wait either! You have a great trip!"

"I will. Meeting an Air Force colonel. Come to think of it. He's from Shreveport, Louisiana, just like your husband. Dan was in the Air Force, right? I bet the Colonel knows Dan. I'm gonna ask him. Now you have a great day!"

"Ok, Clebe, I certainly will. Stay safe, and I guess we'll see you soon."

I hung up the phone with a wonderful feeling that Dan and I would soon have two new friends. One story, 30 years, and now a friendship. God certainly works in strange ways ... and on His own timetable!

Almost Perfect Love Story

Thy will be done. It is not for us to question why or to know the answer. As Christians we are asked to accept His will, to give Him our love, to thank and praise Him, and to believe in His wisdom, thus strengthening our faith, even in troubled times.

Every woman dreams of her perfect love story. Handsome fiance, beautiful wedding, devoted husband, wonderful kids. All that and much more had been mine. And then, one day, the marriage ended.

The first hint the marriage might end came one day in the hospital lobby where I was waiting for my husband, David, to get out of surgery. He was having a lump removed that was visible under his ear and extending to his jaw line. I wasn't overly concerned. Doctors and our dentist had examined him and no one had raised any red flags, at least not to me. This was simply a procedure to remove a nuisance of a cyst. Our twenty-two year old son, DJ, was waiting with me in the lobby reserved for family and friends of those who were having surgery. Our wait had already been lengthy, and I admit I was getting a little nervous.

The doctor was upon me before I even noticed his entrance. He motioned me to a table and we sat down. "Mrs. Shymansky, I'll be honest. It doesn't look good. We've taken a sample of the cyst and are sending it out for a biopsy. I'm going to admit David overnight for observation. I'll have the biopsy report in the morning, and then all of us will sit down and talk. I'm going to make the arrangements to have him admitted. You can spend the night here with him. Someone will come and get you soon. I'll see you in the morning." And with a pat on my hand, he was gone. Never had the C word been mentioned, but it reminded me of when I saw my first coyote. I'd never seen a live coyote, and I didn't expect to see one strolling past the fence line on my Virginia farm that day, but I knew in an instant that it *was* a coyote. The doctor was talking about cancer.

I am ashamed to admit that I went into shock. I crawled into my son's lap and began crying. I've lived with that shame all this time, and I am telling you now, DJ, how sorry I am that I wasn't stronger for *you* in that moment. In my defense, I was appalled that cancer could possibly find its way into my Marine Corps, police officer husband. Six foot 6½ inch, 250-pound handsome hunks who never smoked do NOT get cancer, even if they did serve two tours of duty in Vietnam, where the use of Agent Orange was prevalent. Loving husbands and incredible fathers who have been happily married for 24 years do not suddenly get cancer. This wasn't possible.

In the next few moments, I did two things. I did what every daughter does when she's troubled; I called my mom and told her what the doctor had said. Then I went to the hospital chapel, fell to my knees and prayed. "Please, Lord, hear my prayer! Lord, I know that Your will be done, but if you could allow this disease to pass us by, I would be forever grateful."

That didn't happen. I spent the night in the hospital with David, and in the morning we got the news from the doctor. "I got the lab report back on the biopsy, and it isn't good news. It's squamous cell carcinoma, the cancer that infects soft tissue. It apparently began at the base of your tongue, David, and progressed from there. We believe it has invaded the lymph nodes in your neck, but we're going to do exploratory surgery to see just how extensive the invasion has been. We'll take the infected lymph nodes out. But first, we're going to set you up for radiation treatments for the next four weeks. We might shrink the cancer that way. You should know, David, cancer comes in stages. The stages identify how far the cancer has likely progressed. Your cancer is stage four."

David spoke for the first time. "How bad is stage four?"

The doctor looked directly at David when he answered. "It's the worst. It means the cancer has spread significantly from the original site."

This was worse news than either of us had anticipated. We reached for each other's hands at the same moment, each of us searching for strength from the other. "Okay, then. I guess we have a fight on our hands, and I hope you're up to the challenge!" was David's only response.

The drive home was fairly quiet, each of us deep in thought as we attempted to digest the devastating news. I remember silently praying, on the ride home, for David's full recovery from the disease, and for strength for us both as he began the journey back to good health. Since God had seen fit to allow the cancer to happen, perhaps He would allow David to recover. We were certainly going to do our part!

But God chose not to answer that prayer, either. David fought with every ounce of his being over the next 26 months, but the onslaught into his soft tissue continued and grew despite two radiation treatments a day for several weeks and many, many months of chemotherapy. The cancer would disappear in one place, only to reappear somewhere else. Finally, it invaded his lungs. After all the treatments, my husband was a weakened shell, falling to just above 90 pounds. Through it all our sons, myself, his sister, brother, sister-in-law, my sister and my mom became caretakers, watching over him, praying for him, making him comfortable, but the day came when he realized that the battle was almost over, and that he had lost.

    I remember it well. The cancer doctor told me that morning that, in his opinion, David had less than a month to live, but I had just been told by our new oncologist that David was to start a new round of chemotherapy! I shared that with the doctor and, between the sobs, told him I didn't want David to pass sick from chemotherapy. If he was about to die, I wanted him to have a chance to rest and pass in peace. The doctor agreed that further treatment was unnecessary and was kind enough to contact hospice for me. That afternoon, I told David that a nurse would be coming to help us and that he wouldn't have to go through all the fuss and bother and pain of dressing for doctor visits and riding to the doctor's office. The doctor would be coming to us from now on until he got stronger. His job was to rest, eat, and begin building himself back up. That evening he dragged himself into the bathroom. I was never very far, and when he whispered my name, I was there.

    He was standing before the mirror, looking at himself. "I'm dying, aren't I?"

    In that moment, my heart broke, and though it has been 16 years since his death, it has never fully healed.

"Why would you say that, David? You're no worse than you have been. You just need to eat more and rest to get your strength back. Your doctor doesn't want you exerting yourself any more than you have to."

He stared intently at me and then shuffled silently to the bed. Later that night, when I was wrapped snugly in his arms, he whispered, "I'm not ready to leave you. I love you so much."

"Then keep fighting, damn it! I need you and love you. You're my hero and my husband and my best friend. That's a hole too big to leave me with! Just get better and stay with me."

"I want to, honey, but I don't think I can. I'm tired, really tired."

In the ensuing days, the hospice nurse began her routine, visiting every other day. The doctor came once a week. David was put on oxygen 24/7, his morphine was increased, and every day he spent a bit more time sleeping. He was getting ready for death; I was getting ready for a miracle. Every day found me praying. "Please God, let David get his appetite back today." "Please God, let David have a pain-free day." "Please God, let David feel stronger today." None of those things happened, and you would think that I would be angry at God for refusing to answer any of my prayers. But strangely enough, above all else, each day found me grateful to Him for giving me one more day with the man I loved. I realized, eventually, that David was going on a journey, one he had prepared for all his life. How could I be unhappy when I knew that David was going to heaven and would spend eternity with the Lord? Isn't that what every Christian lives for? That thought kept me strong and helped me survive the loss I was about to experience.

One evening, two of our sons, DJ and Cory, and David's sister, brother and sister-in-law were all sitting with me in David's bedroom. David had been sleeping most of the evening. Suddenly, he was wide awake and pointing toward the window. "Turn out the light," he spoke in a weak, raspy voice. "It's too bright! It's hurting my eyes!" Even though it was night time, and there was no light on in the bedroom except the tiny lamp at the bedside, we all turned and looked at the window. As expected, there was no light coming through the closed blinds, not even a hint. David was sitting up now, his arm shielding his eyes. "Please, please go away. Make the light go away," he spoke in an anguished voice, and then he fell back onto the bed and into a deep sleep. Those of us in the room were almost afraid to speak. I'm not certain what the others thought, but I am convinced the angels came for David that night. He didn't go willingly though, because he was still with us the next morning, though he was barely breathing and unresponsive. However, at 6:09 AM, the exact birth time of his oldest son, David exhaled his final breath, and our marriage ended.

To say I was brokenhearted is an understatement. The moment he took his final breath, I began missing him. I miss him still. But even in the throes of the anguish and heartbreak, there was a deeper feeling inside me. There was joy. It wasn't joy for me; it was joy for David. For 26 months, I had watched him suffer. I had witnessed his pain, his grief, his frustration and, finally, his acceptance. Now he was beyond all that. His only experience for the rest of eternity would be one of joy so bountiful, the human mind is incapable of imagining it, and for that I was grateful. I was grateful that his mother had introduced him to the Lord. I was grateful that he had experienced a personal relationship with the Lord as he was growing into that brave, honorable, loving man. And I was thankful and humbled that God had chosen me to be David's partner. Though we didn't have a lifetime together the way a perfect love story would, the time we did have was a blessing. So, how could I be angry at God? God's will had been done, and my job was to seek comfort from Him and continue to thank him every day of my life for having loaned David to me in the first place. My life is richer and more blessed for having been his wife.

A Love Letter to Cobb Island

God will take you to physical places that touch your heart and your soul. They are meant to remind you of Him, His power, and His goodness. They are special blessings from Him to you. Thank Him when you get there!

Dear Cobb Island,

Do you know how incredibly important places are in people's lives? You, for instance, have been in my life since I was given life. I have spent part of every year since my birth with you and more time than that when my grandparents moved here. I was with them the day they first picked out their new house. Little did I suspect that, even then, you were working your magic on me to bring me home. I was merely anticipating spending summers with my beloved grandparents, but you had other plans. Eventually, you gave me one of your finest sons to love and treasure, and you became more than just the place I lived. You became the home of my heart in every way.

Home... That word evokes images that will forever look and sound and smell like you. Wherever I go, I will take the intense beauty of your sunrises and sunsets with me. I will hear the chatter of the osprey and the cry of the gulls, and I will know I am home. Nowhere I travel will ever have a more poignant scent than yours. My favorite smell of you is from my early years. I remember the salty-sweet aroma of river spray being blown over sun-dried oyster shells, then wafting slowly through pink-flowered mimosa trees. The scent blew gently to me as I perched in the upstairs window at Uncle Jess's house, just down the street from where I sit writing this. Each time I listen to the gentle caressing of waves upon the beach, I will think of the countless nights that sound lulled me to sleep through my open bedroom window. Forever etched in my heart is every step of the many miles I walked up and down your streets. They are safe and friendly and offer a myriad of relaxing sights. Much tension has been released here and many problems solved as I walked my way to serenity. Thank you for that.

From the moment I first met you, I'm sure I fell in love. Each passing year and new memory only deepened the emotion. My sons were born here; you raised them well. They love you as I do, for you gave them a safe haven, a beautiful place to live, and numerous friends and family members we all hold dear. I can never repay you for what you have given me; I only hope that the time I spent here, in some way, made you a little better, too.

Now, it's time for me to leave. New chapters in my life have to be written. It is never easy to leave what you love, but sometimes the past keeps us from facing the future, and while you and I have a past rich with blessings, it has also been fraught with great pain, the greatest pain of my life. I fear I must move on to actually alleviate the remaining pain and enjoy the most recent blessing you sent me, my new husband. Your magic lured him here, too, and you saved him for me.

So, this is goodbye, though I will return frequently, I'm sure. After all, I am leaving behind one son, a daughter-in-law and a grandson to take my place. Work your magic; bring them blessings. Thank you for all my friends, for all my family, and for the beauty. I love you.

Sincerely,

Sharon Shymansky Roberts

Along for the Ride

When God places an opportunity in front of you, by all means, pray about it, but don't let fear keep you from taking it on. Fear is the opposite of faith. Fear will keep your feet tied to the ground; faith will give you wings and show you how to fly!

A few weeks ago I enjoyed a leisurely tractor ride as I mowed one of our fields. The morning was crisp with just the right mixture of sunshine and breeze. Far from the jingling of the phone and the myriad responsibilities awaiting me, I plowed along in mindless comfort, thanking God for leading me to this opportunity to do just what I was doing. Suddenly a grasshopper, against all odds, landed squarely on the hood of my John Deere. From his vantage point high atop the tractor, he surveyed his entire world, a view he had probably never seen and might never be afforded again. As he stayed with me for most of the ride, I could not help but ponder the similarities between that grasshopper and myself. (It seems early morning tractor rides bring out the philosopher in me. Who knew?)

What had inspired this grasshopper to make such a gigantic leap? While the other grasshoppers were making short, frantic sideways jumps to avoid the onslaught of the tractor tires, this grasshopper, without benefit of reason, took a leap of faith and ended up far above his peers, enjoying a sight and a ride they would likely never experience.

I am 55. I have led a grasshopper life, jumping from school to school for teaching assignments over my 29 years in education. Now, when I am admittedly in the throes of menopause (and in serious need of psychiatric counseling if you ask my sons and my mom), I make a leap of faith, just like the grasshopper, and end up on the ride of my life. I am a new alpaca rancher.

How that grasshopper must have felt riding that tractor, moving along effortlessly, faster than he had ever moved before, in directions he had never taken, to places he had never seen! He must have been exhilarated and excited and a little afraid. How like that grasshopper I am. It has been a whirlwind ride this year. In twelve months my husband and I sold our waterfront home, bought land, built a new home and a barn, fenced in some of our 13+ acres, searched for and bought our foundation herd, found a vet with camelid experience, found a feed source, learned about and bought hay, researched our soil... and the list goes on. I can barely take in all the changes. No longer a teacher – I am a business owner, a rancher. Who ever imagined that now, with my life half over, at a time when most people retire and move to slower paced lifestyles, I would take this direction?

But if you were to ask me my feelings, they would mirror those I imagine the grasshopper had. I am exhilarated by the newness of it all. Every day I learn something more about alpacas, fiber or spinning, and the teacher in me is still thrilled by learning. I am excited to have these wonderful, gentle animals to care for and share my home with, and excited also by the prospect of being able to introduce others to God's most perfect livestock. I mean, really, not only are they soft and furry with huge brown eyes that will melt your heart, not only do they make the most adorable humming sound when they are happy, but they also have community poop piles! How awesome is that?

Yes, I am afraid of taking on this new venture, but each day lessens those fears as I grow in confidence and faith that God has led us to this moment. At first I was afraid of the financial commitment and the risk. What if we never sold an alpaca? Now, I feel confident the likelihood of that happening is small. Besides, even if we never did sell an alpaca, how is that bad? We will have gained wonderful two-legged and four-legged friendships in the alpaca world and a new home in a peaceful valley that we get to share with our alpacas. We will get to experience births, alpaca kisses, and the frolicking of the youngsters. Each morning my husband and I will look out at our fields dotted with alpacas and feel proud of what we have accomplished as the autumn of our years approaches. Not a bad life.

Yes, like the grasshopper, I am definitely along for the ride and enjoying the sights and life only the boldest grasshoppers will ever enjoy. May you also take a leap of faith when given a chance. Trust in God and know that you are where you are supposed to be.

This story was written eleven years ago, at the start of our alpaca adventure. We enjoyed the farm life for ten years and never regretted the opportunity for a moment. In fact, life would have been a bit dull if we hadn't trusted God to take us on that journey. Now, both retired, we took another leap of faith and moved to Pawleys Island, SC, to give island life a try. So far, all I can say is, God is good, very, very good!

The Power of Faith, Family and Friends

Sometimes there is tragedy. God never promised us an easy life free of toil and trouble. He did, however, promise us life everlasting with Him in heaven. But first we need to seek Him, even in our darkest times, for He is there with us.

5:35 a.m. Thursday morning. The alarm had just gone off. I remember Dan slapping the snooze button and then turning and wrapping me snugly in his arms for a moment or two. That comforting, secure feeling shattered with the intruding shrill of the telephone. Early morning phone calls are seldom good news. Dan answered, but I heard the speaker's words clearly and was out of bed and dressing before the caller had finished her message.

Cory, my middle son, had been in a car accident. It was bad. The caller instructed us to start for the hospital, but felt Cory would probably be flown to Med Star, the shock trauma unit at Washington Hospital Center in DC. She'd stay in contact with us on the cell phone. Hurry!

In an instant I was thrust into a mother's worst nightmare. Though I am a strong woman, when life comes at you that quickly, hurtling the real possibility of a son's death upon you, strength eludes you. At least it did me. I didn't fall apart; I didn't sob hysterically. I was just laid bare, right to my soul, helpless, defeated, afraid. For an instant, there was numbness… and then… I began praying. I prayed that no one else had been involved, and if they had, that they lived. I prayed for my son and for his son. I prayed for his brothers, and I prayed for strength for me. As we climbed into the truck to make the 35-minute drive to the hospital, I reached into the glove compartment for my husband's rosary, and I began saying the Hail Mary. Once, I glanced out the window and noticed the shrouding fog, the worst fog I ever remembered seeing, and I knew at least one of the reasons for the accident. The fog kept us creeping at a snail's pace, but throughout the trip, I continued praying the Rosary. I'd like to reassure you that prayer kept me strong, but I'd be lying. Prayer kept me busy, and it kept me hoping, but my insides were beginning to tighten and twist painfully. It's rather strange that you can spend an entire life never really knowing terror, yet the moment it lodges inside you, you recognize it instantly. Terror was the predominant feeling inside the truck cab, and only prayer kept it from suffocating me.

At the hospital, the nightmare became stark reality. Family and friends began pouring into the waiting room, and details of the accident began leaking through the numbness and escalating the terror. Head trauma. Unresponsive. Punctured lung. Skull and neck fractures. 45 minutes before he was found. Each additional detail added to the bleak picture, and I understood that prayer was truly the only thing I could do for my son, so I did it well. From the depths of my heart I prayed to Mother Mary. I knew she would understand the love a mother bears for her child, how no other love on earth is quite like it, and how heart wrenching the possibility of losing a son is. Even more importantly, for the first time in my life, I felt like I really knew and understood her pain. I kept praying. It occurred to me, during that early morning vigil, that if it hadn't been for my mom taking me to church and introducing me to my Lord, I would not have been able to do even this for my son. Thank you, Mom. I remember wondering briefly what people who have not formed a personal relationship with God do for comfort and hope when they find themselves in tragic situations. I cannot imagine not having Him to turn to. About that time, our monsignor showed up, was admitted into the sacred halls of the emergency room, and gave a special anointing to my son. God had truly been informed – we wanted this young man saved! The number in the waiting room was quietly growing. Each passing minute seemed to bring a new family member or friend through the doors. I had called my sister as soon as I had gotten the news, and she dropped whatever plans she had for the morning and drove through the terrible fog to sit with me. My sister-in-law, brother-in laws, cousins, aunts, uncles, nieces, nephews raced to the hospital as the day dawned. Cory's friends did as well. It seems humorous now, but the hospital staff called for a backup security guard, the numbers had grown so large. Quietly I glanced from face to face, and my burden was lifted a little. It was very obvious I was not alone in my fear and that knowledge, somehow, made fear easier to bear. First prayer, now family and friends. I was beginning to feel very blessed, even in the midst of this tragic event.

And then the news. He was alive, but he desperately needed to be transported to shock trauma. He couldn't be flown because of the fog and transporting by ambulance was risky. But, there was no choice. He had to go. I begged a ride in the front seat of the ambulance, and we were on our way.

Even there, faith, family and friends rode along. His cousin was on the hospital staff, and she sat at his head, gently comforting him, explaining to him, even though we were certain he could hear nothing. Friends from the rescue squad sat in attendance and another drove. I kept up the prayer vigil. It was a very long ride.

Shock trauma was both the height of the nightmare and the home of the angels. It was there I was allowed my first close look at my son. His face laid open to the bone in several places, the bloody, gashed head, the eyes swollen shut, the blood-stained neck collar, the tubes in both lungs, the ventilator to keep him breathing. My son was in the fight of his life, and I was helpless. Humbling. Very humbling. No matter how much we think we are in control, we aren't.

Quickly, efficiently, but compassionately, the doctors and nurses worked for hours on my son. In the end, God saved him, but their hands and minds were the instruments through which He worked. Meanwhile, the trauma waiting room was filling up. Even though the hospital was over an hour away from home and rush hour traffic was in full swing, family and friends came to wait. At one point there were more than 30 people spilling out of the small waiting area into the hallway. My heart was full; even if the worst happened, I would not be alone.

But the best happened. My son, who had sped straight into a brick church (the irony is not lost on me, I guarantee you) wearing no seat belt – who lay enveloped by the fog for 45 minutes in his blood and vomit amid glass and bricks under a roof which miraculously did not collapse on him; who suffered a fractured skull a hairsbreadth away from his spinal cord; two fractured vertebrae in his neck millimeters from his arterial artery; a fractured face that stopped miraculously short of his orbital socket; a nose shattered clear through the septum and laid wide open; a pierced lung and another that had to be pierced to drain the fluid that was filling them both up; a broken rib right over his heart – this son was wheeled out of the hospital just seven days later. While he still has much rehabilitation in front of him, this son should not have lived. Look at his truck; look at the church; look at the pictures they took of him at the hospital. He was dying, but he was saved. Why? I don't know why; that is not ours to know. But I wholeheartedly believe God saved him for a purpose, and I pray every day that Cory opens his heart and listens, for God will be trying to show him the reason and guide him to a greater life than he has ever enjoyed, I have no doubt. How was he saved? That's easy. The power of faith, the power of family, and the power of friends.

We have those powers within us. At any moment, on any given day, we are encouraged to turn to the Lord and offer up our prayers, our troubles, our hopes, our joys, our wants. We are invited to invoke the power through our faith. Each day, as members of an earthly family, we have the power to lift up someone simply because we are bound together by human ties. United, a family is a powerful force. Finally, there is the power of friendship. Friends are the people we choose to allow into our inner sanctums; we tell them our fears and our dreams, and we trust they will support and love us for who we are, not because they have to as members of our family, but because they want to as members of our inner circle. Each of us is a friend, and that relationship with another individual is both precious and powerful; it carries a great obligation to use that power wisely for the good of our friends. You see, each of us is a powerful individual. Together, our individual powers can make miracles. Cory is living proof, and I am a grateful eye witness.

It is my prayer that family and friends know how much we appreciate the time you spent with us when we needed you most. May you understand that the love you shared by taking time from your own lives to spend time with us in our darkness, that your words, your hugs, your kindnesses to Cory and our family all helped give us strength to face the future and helped heal my son's body and soul. When he felt the outpouring of love, he had no choice but to get better. I know he is thanking each of you in his own way as he works through his convalescence. This thanks is mine, from a mother's heart. I am forever indebted to each of you, and I love you all. For everything you did, thank you. And finally, to my mom who introduced me to my Lord. She led me to the altar and to the Bible. Where I took that knowledge and experience is my story, but she gave me the opportunity to develop my own personal relationship with the Lord. It is that relationship, sinner though I am, that sustains me during the hard times, that lifts me up and gives me hope for the future. I do not know how anyone survives life's trials without knowing Him in an intimate and personal way. I continuously work on improving my own relationship with Him, and even though I fail more than I succeed, I still try. I pray that my sons continue to seek Him and to build their own relationships with Him for their benefit, and for the benefit of those they love, especially my grandchildren.

This story was first published in May, 2015, in the book, *Shorts*, which is a compilation of a variety of writings by members of Beach Author's Network.

Alpacas and... Dragonflies?

God has given me an adventurous spirit. I am not afraid to take chances, because I trust He has a plan for me. So when I met and fell in love with the first alpaca I ever saw, I had a pretty good idea God was telling me it was time to sell my waterfront home and my jet skis, and look for a farm. I was in my mid-50s at the time. My sons called it menopause gone bad; I called it an adventure! Luckily, I am blessed with a husband who is equally adventurous, so we started our journey together.

"So, why alpacas?" everyone asks. "Do they come when you call them?"

*Umm. Well, they **have** names. I call them by their names all the time, and sometimes they look my way when I call them but, mostly, when I have a bucket of grain in my hands.*

"Do they show you affection? Do they love you?"

*Umm. Well, they do show me affection, some of them, a couple of them, actually, one of them **really** shows affection... to everyone who comes to visit! And I read once where they remember you for six months after they have moved to another farm. But... after six months... you're history – literally!*

Truthfully, I care more about what my alpacas have brought to my life than what I have brought to theirs. I bring them much: a regular feeding program of top-quality grain and hay, fresh water daily, a roof over their heads if they want one, guard dogs to keep them safe, regimented healthcare, a smiling face if they happen to glance my way, and unconditional love, even when they spit. But they bring me more, and what they bring isn't measured by dollars as some entrepreneurs might suggest. It's measured in joy, and that's truly *immeasurable*.

Alpacas have brought me pride. Who knew my husband and I could design and build a barn? Not me! Who knew we could fence in five acres, and then another six? Not me! Who knew I would be able to give shots, deliver babies, scoop poop, drive a tractor? Never, never, never me. But... oh yes I can, and do, and, the kicker is – I love it!

Alpacas have brought me something to do I truly love. I love taking care of them. I love planning the breedings, deciding who should be mated with whom, what each will bring to the offspring. I love the birthing, even if I do forget to breathe for just a while when that nose first starts poking out. I love the smell of hay, the chomping sounds as they munch grain, the sight of alpaca babies (cria) and their moms bouncing (pronking) through the fields. I love tiptoeing into the barn early in the morning and catching them sleepy-eyed. I love to see them play with one another, show affection to one another, nurse their cria, strut their stuff for their women. I love this life alpacas have brought me. Thank God I had this chance.

Alpacas have provided me another outlet for my "cria-tivity." Once I felt the softness of spun alpaca fiber, I knew spinning was something I would learn to do. Several hours into the first spinning lesson, I remember the instructor yelling at me in exasperation, "Can't you feel it? Can't you feel what that fiber wants to do? Stop holding it back!" The lesson finally ended. She gave me a large pile of roving to take home to spin, and confided to her husband, unbeknownst to me, that she was certain she would never see me again. Sometime around 11 o'clock that night, I felt it, and the feeling brought goosebumps. It does even now as I recall it. One moment I was "lumping" my way through the pile; the next, my fiber began drafting smoothly through my fingers, and I knew what she was talking about. I merely had to stop forcing my will onto the fiber and let it twist its own way into that wonderful yarn. (Is there a Biblical lesson here? If we listened to Him more often instead of forcing our will into our daily lives, maybe we'd be living even happier lives according to His original plan for us!) I arrived at my teacher's home early the next morning, the entire pile of roving spun into respectable yarn. She greeted me at the door in astonishment. When she looked into the basket and saw what I had produced, she smiled openly and said, "Welcome, spinner. Let's go make some more yarn!"

    Oh, and one more thing alpacas have brought me. Dragonflies. As my husband and I toiled in the fields today putting up more fencing, the dragonflies were everywhere. Do you have any idea how many color combinations they come in? If alpacas are nature's most color diverse animals (and they are), dragonflies have got to be number one in the insect world. Greens. Blues. Yellows. Patterns. They are gorgeous! Out of nowhere one landed on my hand, and I wasn't even holding a bucket of grain! If it weren't for alpacas, I wouldn't have been in the right place at the right time to have a dragonfly land on my fingers and stay a while to watch me. I would never have known how lightly, how softly, they sit on your skin. I would never have understood the word "gossamer" as well as I understand it now that I've gazed through a dragonfly wing. "Dragonfly" would have remained just a word in a dictionary.

So, thank you, God, for the adventurous spirit You placed within me, for giving me the courage to take on new adventures, and for giving me a joyful nature to love them all!

Tourist Eyes

We are exactly where we are meant to be at any given time. What we do when we get there is our free will, a gift from God.

A dreary, rainy day found my husband and I in the car on our way to explore some Pawleys Island shops. The quiet induced by the lull of the rain shattered as Dan blurted out, "Even though we've only lived in Pawleys since December, promise me we won't ever lose our 'tourist eyes'!"

"Huh?" (I mean, really, where had **that** come from?)

"You know, that sense of wonder and excitement and eagerness tourists have when they're visiting a new place. Promise me, no matter how long we live here, we won't ever lose it. Pawleys is such a special place, and we are so fortunate to finally be living here. We can't ever take her for granted."

The ensuing "tourist eyes" discussion left me feeling a bit guilty. Was it possible that after only seven months here, I had already started to take for granted all Pawleys had to offer? Getting out of the car at the next group of shops, I decided to go in with tourist eyes wide open. I carefully explored every shelf, peeked into every nook and corner, spoke to every store owner and had a grand time. Nothing amazed me as much, however, as what I found in a small shop next to a deli where I had eaten several times.

In the back of the shop, a gentleman was bent over a table working with a variety of beads. My outgoing, nosey-to-a-fault attitude suddenly emerged. "What are you doing?"

"Making blessing bracelets."

"Blessing bracelets? What are they?"

"Oh," answered the man's wife, "they are bracelets we have created made from a variety of Swarovski pearls and crystals. Each pearl represents a blessing in your life. When you wear the bracelet, touch each pearl, think about a blessing you have been given, and send God a prayer of thanks for each one. Just watch your life change as you count your blessings!"

What a wonderful way to remind myself to thank God for all the blessings he has bestowed on me. I don't do that as often as I should. And to find them birthed and handmade right here in Pawleys! How wonderful is that? So, I bought one, and it works! Each time I slip it on my wrist, I religiously start counting and thanking. It's like an obligation I feel compelled to fulfill, and it makes me feel good. (I've already returned to purchase more for gifts. I know people who have so much and who continue to focus on what they don't have! How sad!)

While I suppose it wouldn't be right to mention the store, let me just say how much the Island Shops brightened that dreary day and how grateful I was to my husband for opening my "tourist eyes"! Who knew a rainy day would end with me feeling still closer to my Lord? Let me go get that bracelet; that's one more blessing to count!

Expect the Unexpected

When I attend mass, I expect to have my faith deepened through the homily. I expect to hear some small message in the lectors' readings that gives me an "aha" moment. I expect to sing and to pray. But what I don't expect is to have God slap my hands and remind me that only He can pass judgment.

I was thrilled to be attending the Lenten mission with my husband. Last year, I had made only one night of the mission, and I had made that one alone. I was determined to attend all three nights this year with my husband by my side. It was night one of the mission, and there I sat, next to my husband, eagerly anticipating the message I would soon be hearing from one of my favorite visiting priests. I must confess to being nerd-like when I am listening to a speaker and enjoying the experience. I was sitting almost on the edge of the pew throughout Father's lecture, pretty much oblivious to everyone and everything around me. The mission ended for the night, we stood for prayers, sang a hymn, and exited the church. As Dan and I were walking to the car, I was excitedly sharing with him all the inspired thoughts that were jumping around in my brain as a result of the lecture. Suddenly, Dan interrupted me.

"You mean to tell me you never saw the guy in front of us who was texting on his phone throughout the whole lecture?" Dan asked in a perturbed voice.

"What? Are you serious? Why in the world would someone come to the mission and spend their entire time texting? What a waste! He might as well have stayed home," I responded.

Dan continued, "I'm telling you, that's exactly what he did, and it's just rude. It's rude to the speaker and it's rude to those of us sitting around him. It was very distracting for me."

"You're right. I'm sorry, honey. I really am. Maybe tomorrow night you'll have a better time." Inside I was praying he would come with me the next night.

The next day promised to be interesting as I had an appointment with a new dentist. Can I just say that on my list of the top 10 things I would rather *not* do, going to the dentist is number one. But it's an important necessity. I had searched the church bulletin weeks before for a dentist, picked one, and immediately asked everyone about him. He got nothing but high praise, so I felt pretty confident I had made a good choice. As expected, everyone at the office was very nice, very welcoming, very soothing. Soon I was in the chair under the skillful hands of the dental assistant, having x-rays taken, answering questions, getting prepared to meet my new dentist for the first time. He arrived shortly, and he seemed vaguely familiar. Where had I seen him? Since he was a parishioner, it seemed logical to assume I had seen him at mass.

He introduced himself and began chatting with me. "I understand you picked me because you and I go to the same church. Is that right?" he asked.

"That's right. We moved here a little over a year ago and we've been going to that church every weekend. We love it there!" I answered.

As he was preparing the tools for his onslaught into my mouth, he kept the dialogue going. "So, did you happen to go to last night's mission? The priest is a good friend of mine. He's been coming here for years, and I really enjoy him. I always learn something new from him."

As I began responding to his question, he put on his glasses, and I had a sudden sinking feeling. I did recognize him. He had been sitting right in front of us in church the previous night at the mission. Please God, don't let this be the texting man that had so annoyed Dan!

"I really enjoyed Father's lecture last night," he continued. "I spent the whole time taking notes on my phone. It just seems that no matter how many times I listen to him, I hear something brand new, or in a way that I've never heard it before, and I don't want to forget it. I want to read it and reread it when I'm alone, so it can really sink in."

Oh boy. There it was! God's smack on my hands. Innocently enough, both Dan and I had judged this God-loving man standing beside me. We had assumed he'd been texting and paying no attention to the lecture. We had judged him to be a disinterested participant, when he had actually been paying a tremendous compliment to the priest. And now here he stood with a long, sharp needle dripping Novocain, ready to puncture the inside of my mouth. Dare I confess to him what Dan and I had thought and said about him to one another?

I am many things, but I am not a fool.

So, I guess my message is to expect the unexpected, even in church. God never gives up on us; He never stops molding and shaping us, even when we are in the right place and supposedly doing the right things. Isn't that just like our Father?

P.S. Dan and I did make it to all three nights of the mission and are so glad we did. By the way, the next Sunday Dan saw one of our ushers "texting" on his phone during the homily, and guess what? He was taking notes! We certainly are a spirit-filled congregation, and I, for one, just need to get rid of my trusty notepad and pen and start using my phone!

If He Calls… Answer!

At some point in your life, I absolutely believe God will call you to be His instrument. He will seek to use you in a way you might never have been expecting, and you will either answer His call or reject it. But I warn you, He doesn't come with a caller ID, so be ready.

Her name was Sandra. I spent only five minutes with her, yet left the encounter deeply changed.

It was a sunshine-perfect summer Sunday on Pawleys Beach – breeze blowing, waves rushing, people swimming and laughing. Umbrellas, coolers, beach chairs and their owners had taken up residence on every speck of sand. My husband and I were people-watching from our beach chairs. I noticed her approach first because of her elegance. Wearing a cream-colored pants suit and dressy sandals, she held herself erect as she walked briskly to the water's edge. With the rest of the beach crowd in bathing suits and cover ups, she was an anomaly. I remember thinking, "She must have come right from church." After my initial observation, I returned my gaze to the myriad of people challenging the surf, but something whispered, "Look again. Look closer." I did.

She was crying, and she was praying. Her hands were clenched in front of her, head bowed, shoulders gently shaking. I remember saying aloud, "Oh, Dan, she's crying," and before I knew what happened, something catapulted me from the sanctity of my beach chair. As if pulled by a magnetic force, I approached her. I remember thinking, "What am I doing? The beach is full of people! I don't know this woman! She's praying; I can't interrupt her praying!" But I did.

I gently touched her shoulder, startling her. "I'm so sorry!" I apologized quickly. "But I noticed you crying, and praying, and I know that wherever two or more persons are gathered in His name, He is there. I thought I could pray with you... for you. May I do that?" My heart was pumping furiously. Loudly! I'd never done anything like this before. Here I stood on the beach in front of all these people asking a stranger if I could pray with her. What in the world had gotten into me? Whatever it was, it was strong. For a moment, she looked at me questioningly, as if she hadn't quite understood me. Tears tracked erratically down her beautiful, ebony face.

"Oh, please," she answered, her voice quivering, head nodding assent.

I gently took her hand. "What's your name?"

"Sandra," she whispered.

I tucked Sandra's arm in mine, pulling us closer together, and with heads bowed, I softly spoke a prayer for her. I don't remember all that I asked of Him, but I know it was heartfelt. After our "Amens" were said, Sandra turned to me. "What's your name?" she asked quietly.

"Sharon."

"Thank you, Sharon. Thank you for standing with me and praying." Her tears had stopped. She looked closely at me, as if searching my soul, smiled beatifically, and hugged me. "I love you, Sharon. May God go with you." And she left.

Looking back, we must have appeared rather strange to the onlookers. The white woman in her bathing suit and the African-American woman in her church clothes standing at the water, arms entwined, praying together. I wonder now what everyone thought.

For whatever reason, God called me that day on Pawleys Beach, and I did His bidding. That is a humbling experience. I left the beach a braver person, one more courageous in expressing her faith in and love for her God. Thank you, Sandra. The experience could have been a much different one. You could have laughed at me, or been rude, or snapped at me in anger, but because of the faith *you* had, I was the one who left enriched.

Lesson learned: We never know when He is going to call on us. Be ready and say "Yes." (Next time, I sincerely hope I am better dressed and 30 pounds lighter if I'm going to have an audience!)

God's Plan

Never doubt that God has a plan for you. He does, and every now and then He reveals it to you in such crystal clear fashion that you would have to be in a coma not to realize it. That's exactly what happened to me. Thankfully, I was not in a coma, but neither was I the only one who recognized God's presence and the work He was doing on my behalf.

I awoke from my night's sleep feeling refreshed, happy, blessed. I finally had a real prayer life going. Prayer isn't something that I do as often as I should. But lately, I've been very consistent about praying every night for those people who have asked for or needed my prayers. I follow those requests by thanking Him for my many blessings, and then I say an Our Father, a Hail Mary and a Glory Be. That's it; I'm done.

I've been consistent now for two months, not missing even one night! Not bad for a 66-year-old woman, huh? (Good thing my Father is a forgiving, patient Father!) Anyway, the sun was shining and today felt promising. After a rewarding literacy tutoring session with my students, I walked in my door to find my husband, Dan, dressed up and waiting for me.

"Hey, cutie! What are you all dressed up for?" I queried.

"I thought I'd take my beautiful wife to a really nice lunch on the ocean."

"Wow! I'm ready!" You'd think when you live at the beach you would do this sort of thing all the time. But, when you live at the beach and you are retired, that retirement income often doesn't stretch to cover frequent oceanfront meals. This was a real treat.

As we walked to the car, he followed behind me and opened my door before I could reach for it. Ah, I know what you're thinking now. No, he wasn't in trouble and was making it up to me, and no, he hadn't been "stepping out" on me. When you've lived a certain amount of ups and downs together and can still take one another's breath away with a look, then you just know that no one is going to come between you. But I was impressed by his chivalry. As we drove out of our development, it was obvious he had a plan in mind. Sure enough, we flew single mindedly down Highway 17 and eventually turned right toward Surfside Beach. A few more turns and we entered the parking lot of a quaint little café sitting on the beach, snuggled sweetly between high-rise condos. It was lovely.

The hostess seated us, gave us menus, and left. Though our attention was torn between gazing at the ocean and the menu, we eventually made our selections. Our waitress arrived. She was pleasant, helpful, and seemed to really enjoy her job. Soon I heard her talking to a man and a woman who sat across the small aisle from us. Snatches of their conversation reached me, sounding like they were talking about Virginia, the state we had recently called home. When she revisited our table, I asked her.

"Did I hear you say you used to live in Virginia?"

"Yes, I did. I lived near Bluefield, but I moved here about eight years ago. Why? Do you live in Virginia?"

"We did. We moved to South Carolina about a year and a half ago."

"Oh, what part of Virginia?"

"King George. It's right across the bridge from Southern Maryland."

"Oh, I know where you mean. It's pretty there." Then she left us to attend to other customers. That's when the young man from the table across the aisle intervened.

"So you guys are from Virginia, huh? I'm really familiar with that state. I used to work in the DC and Baltimore areas, and we'd sail our boat down the Chesapeake Bay to the Potomac." Then, speaking to Dan, he asked, "What did you do for a job when you were in Virginia?" That led to a lengthy discussion of power plants, electricity, steam, radioactivity, and the earth. By the time that conversation was exhausted, we had all finished our meals, and Dan and I were standing by their table still talking. About that time it became apparent God had a plan, and I was about to be the central figure.

I innocently asked, "So what do you do, John?"

"Well, among other things, I'm a screenplay writer. This is my mom, Sandy. She's an author, and I've just finished the screenplay for her novel."

This might be a good time to mention to you that I've been a closet writer most of my life. Since moving here, I've become involved with an amazing parish community and an inspiring woman's club at the church. As a result, I've been writing and sharing some personal, faith-based essays within our woman's club circle. I have gotten such positive responses from so many people that I have begun to wonder if God is calling me to be a Christian writer. I have prayed about it and asked God to "give me a sign." Nope. Nothing. Not a single sign I can decipher. (It's not nice to test your Lord.)

Dan didn't miss a beat. "Wow! You aren't going to believe this. My wife is the best writer! She is really great. She's written all these stories about..." and he was off on a roll. (Can you tell my husband is my best fan?) I could feel my face flushing with embarrassment, and I began praying for invisibility or for Dan to run out of air, temporarily of course.

"Really?" Sandy said as she turned to me. "Are you published?"

An uncomfortable silence followed **that** question.

"No, I'm not, unless you count our church newsletter, or the community newsletter where I used to live." Humiliated, I lowered my eyes. It's that dreaded question "Are you published?" that seems to imply if you aren't, then you're no good, and if you are, then you're a real writer. "The truth is," I continued, "I'm a coward. I don't think I can go through all the trouble of lovingly crafting a work only to have a publisher reject it. I'm afraid." Raising my gaze to her face, I witnessed an astonished look passing between mother and son.

"Why, Sharon, you need to come to our writers' club meeting next Tuesday," she invited. "My son, John, will be the guest speaker, and he's talking about self-publishing."

John quickly interjected. "That's right. Sharon, you've got to come! Mom and I have spent the past two years researching all the self-publishing niches. We've listened to so many authors who have been victimized by nefarious publishers. We know the ins and outs; we have contacts. We can help you."

"That settles it, Sharon," the woman continued. "You'll join our writing group, and you'll come Tuesday and learn about self-publishing, if that's the route you choose to take. We can get you read. Our writing group members are such a great group of people; they are always encouraging and uplifting."

"I appreciate this. I really do," I heard myself muttering, "but I don't know if there are people in your group who would actually want to read what I feel like I'm being called to write. You see, I think I'm supposed to be a Christian writer."

Another look of astonishment, and then the *ProofThatGodIsInThisRoom* words, "Why... Sharon... I'm also a Christian writer, and I think we have the perfect writer's group for you. Come and see." She handed me her contact information as she spoke. I was speechless. Those of you who know me will find that very hard to believe, but it is true. Oddly, there were tears in my eyes. One thought, only one, resonated inside me. "This is My plan for you."

I found a voice, of sorts, and managed to whisper, "Do you know God is using you right now?" She smiled. But when I turned to Dan, that's when I had confirmation God had been present. He was wide-eyed, his mouth a perfect O, his jaw dropping significantly below its normal elevation.

He was silent until we said our goodbyes and left the restaurant. As we walked to the car, he started, "I can't believe what just happened. You have just started writing again and sharing Christian essays and this happened today?" He was at a loss.

"You know how it happens, Dan. You truly know, don't you?"

He answered without hesitation. "Yeah. I feel like I have just been in His presence. But more than that, I'm totally convinced how much He loves us. To think that He takes the time to work out a plan for each of us and then reveal it in this way is truly mind-blowing, but I just saw the proof!"

Dan has always been a Christian but, on this day, I think he also became a true believer in God's individual plan for each of us. And me? I'm just excited to be on this journey and can't wait to see where it takes me!

Acknowledgments

When you write your first book, there are so many people to thank. People who inspired you. People who supported you. People who loved you. And then there are the people who agreed to read your work and edit it for you, knowing full well that this is your work of love and that you have sweated over it, prayed over it, cried over it. And yet, they agreed to mercilessly edit out all your mistakes and share their impressions of where you could make it better, knowing you would be happier in the end. So let the thank-you's begin.

Thank you…

… Dan, who was so excited I was writing again, he never even minded the hours I spent at the computer, keeping him from doing all the things he wanted to do. It goes without saying, but I'll say it anyway, his incredible faith in my writing ability and his unfailing support were a big part of this book.

… Beach Authors Network (BAN) members who read earlier versions, encouraged me, worked with me, and offered friendships that I truly cherish.

… Pat David, who took my passable poetry and made it truly

"poetic."

… Sandy Springs and her son, John, who invited me to join the writing group. You were truly doing God's work that day.

… Jean and Frank Mudd, dear friends who read everything I wrote, inspired me to keep writing, and then agreed to act as editors. You made this endeavor better, and I love you for it!

… Diane and Steve Boyle, our Camillo Valley Beaver Rescue Club members, who also agreed to edit. Your comments were insightful. I hope I did them justice.

… Clebe McClary, who gave me permission to use the story "The Homecoming" in this book. Meeting him and reading the story aloud to him was one of the most special moments in this writer's life.

… DJ, Cory, and Ryan, my sons, for their support, their love, and their pride in me for finally accomplishing my dream. You are my treasures and my greatest accomplishments.

… Mom, who gave me life and my Lord. In between, and every day, you gave me unconditional love. (Remember always, you were my first love!)

www.ingramcontent.com/pod-product-compliance
Lightning Source LLC
LaVergne TN
LVHW042045070526
838201LV00077B/717